Brent Shaw

DISTILLATIONS

Volume One: Brightest Green

(By Brent Shaw)

Copyright © 2007 by Brent Shaw

Distillations
Volume One: Brightest Green
by Brent Shaw

Printed in the United States of America

ISBN 978-1-60477-129-9

All rights reserved solely by the author. The author guarantees all contents are original and do not infringe upon the legal rights of any other person or work. No part of this book may be reproduced in any form without the permission of the author. The views expressed in this book are not necessarily those of the publisher.

Unless otherwise indicated, Bible quotations are taken from the New American Standard Bible. Copyright © 1973 by Moody Press, Chicago.

www.xulonpress.com

TABLE OF CONTENTS

Cycle One: Nature and Humanity 13

                    Brightest Green 15
                    Sleeping Bee 16
                    The Cat 17
                    Spring With Butterfly 20
                    Shine, Stars! Shine! 21
                    Carcass 22

Cycle Two: Death 25

                    If I Should Die 27
                    Covered In Hearts 28
                    Death 29
                    It Matters Not 30
                    You Must Leave Me Now 32
                    It Is Death 33
                    I Didn't Want To Say Goodbye 34
                    I Was Just Thinking 35

Cycle Three: Virginia Tech., April 16, 2007 37

                    Before They Grew Old 39
                    V.P.I., April 16, 2007 40
                    Mother, Mother 41

Cycle Four:	Family	43
	The Highways and By-Ways	45
	"Got That Happy Right!"	47
	Brenda: Girl With A Twirl!	48
Cycle Five:	Biblical Themes	51
	The Prodigal	53
	Emmaus	54
Cycle Six:	Humor	61
	"Up and Into the Bus!"	62
	"Still Here!"	67
	Move Your Thumb!	71
Cycle Seven:	Christian Living	73
	Praising God	75
	Battling God	76
	Strayed Far	77
	A Lone Tree	78
	Here Am Just I!	79
	It Will Sound Like A Boast	80
Cycle Eight:	God	83
	Mr. Mystery	85
	Omnipresence	86
Cycle Nine:	Nostalgia	87
	The Last Penny	89

Cycle Ten:	Fantasy	91
	The "Solo Maiden"	93
	Just A Wish	94
	Captain of the Seas	95
Cycle Eleven:	Both Sides	99
	Dutch Door	101
	She Dreams/He Dreams	103
	Metal and Mineral	106
Cycle Twelve:	Life	107
	Depression	109
	Time To Go	110
	Orphaned	111
	Do You Suppose...?	112
	Where Do You Sleep?	114
	In A Dream	115
	We Each Have A Closet	116
	My Friends	118
Cycle Thirteen:	Anecdotes	119
	The Most Beautiful Instrument	121
	"The Size Of That Thing!"	122
Cycle Fourteen:	Ways of the World	125
	Making Juice	126
Cycle Fifteen:	Evolution	127
	It Isn't the Same, Now!	129

Cycle Sixteen: Shaped Poems 131

    I Drop 133
    Eve and Adam 134
    Bubbles Of Laughter 135
    Going Backward 136

Cycle Seventeen: Romance 137

    Eternally Yours! 139
    …Only For A Moment? 140
    I Didn't Want To Say Goodbye 141
    Love's Stirring At Sea! 142
    I'll Take This Chance! 143
    I Can't Close My Eyes Again! 144
    Or Am I? And Do I! 145
    It's Lovely Here With You! 146
    Where? 147

Cycle Eighteen: The Rapture 149

    "Light Through Night!" 151
    "Please Come!" 152

Cycle Nineteen: Winter 155

    "It's Cold! Freezing!" 157
    This Christmas Morn 158

Bio Blurb

The writer is a twenty-four-year resident of Farmville, Virginia. He moved there in 1983 in order to attend Longwood College, and live near his twin sister, Brenda. Brent has been diagnosed "bipolar," and is learning to live with this mental illness through medications, counseling, and especially the love and support of his wife, Jo Leslie, and his family in Christ at Faith Bible Fellowship in Farmville (Pastor: Lee Copeland). He intends to produce future volumes of poetry under the escutcheon, "Distillations," and is already hard at work producing Volume Two.

Flyleaf Dedication

To Dad and Mom,
who gave me birth; to
Buzz and Lavon Collis,
who gave me to rebirth in
Christ; to my darling, sweet Jolie,
who gave me the priceless gift of her life.
To God: *Every good gift and every perfect gift*
is from above, and comes down from the Father of lights,
with whom is no variableness, neither shadow of turning. (James
1:17)
Father,
Son,
Spirit,
Trinity!

Cycle One:
Nature and Humanity

Brightest Green

Our brightest green is when we're born:
a throwback to the first acorn!
The bud of body, mind, and soul
Has reached perfection as one whole.

Then darker green, and darker still,
we grow to wonder at the thrill
of living, loving, giving; making
sap and bark in the undertaking.

Nearing death we change to brown;
we fall to lofty autumn down;
the freckled landscape of our past
relents to winter's snowy blast.

But the Gardener will not rest
till He's done His very best:
sowing, watering, nourishing, when—
bursting through the ground again—

Brightest green is brighter still,
just beyond the fruitful Hill!

Sleeping Bee

Never heard of a sleeping bee?
Neither have I!
Yet, what do we know, and what see
of secrets high
On nature's totem-panoply?

We hear the bumbling Bumble-Bee.
We fear the sting
Of yellow jacket, "killer bee,"
Dauber daubing,
Hornet circling threateningly!

We know the busy Honeybee:
queen and worker,
(not the drone) sidles speedily—
not a shirker—
Sends Morse code of the perfect tree

For honeycombs and clover's lee
meadow of swell
blooms! *Apis melliferas*? Gee!
If I could tell
What they smell, feel, and hear softly—

Let alone what they know and see
(or don't...if they
Sleep)—I would pollinate, gladly,
A poem today
For you to grow in a nest's tree!

The Cat

It wants its food,
    and it wants it now!
It feels its mood,
    and it feels it now!

It wants its sleep,
    and it wants it now!
It wants to creep,
    and it wants to now!

It wants its tom,
    and it wants him now!
It wants its "plum,"
    and it wants her now!
It wants its tom;
    it wants its frau;
It wants its sex,
    and it wants it
        NOWoohWOWoohWOWoohWOW...!

It wants its play,
    and it wants it now!
It wants to stay,
    and will do so now!

It wants ol' "Chap"
    to stop, "Bow Wow!"—
to shut his trap,
    and do it now!

It wants to stretch!
    It wants to bow!
It won't just "Fetch!"
    Not then...not now!

It loves to fight...
    to have a row:
Achilles sight
    right here! Right nnnnnnnnnnnOW!

It loves to preen
    after it eats.
Must lick all clean
    before retreats!

It often hunts
    despite the meals
offered in punts
    from "Caveman('s)" heels!

It shuns a kiss,
    and with a hiss!
Its biting bliss
    comes quickly, Sis!

It seeks to hide
    under a bough!
It wants "free ride"
    for living now!

It may do this;
    it may do that!
One thing's amiss
    about the cat:

Cats don't really
    croon a "Meow!"
Silly! Silly!
    Cats all say, "NOW!"

<u>Spring With Butterfly</u>

Ah, Rosebud Petal
   in springtime reverie,
      on whom Butterfly comes to land
         instead of touching me!

Midst bright sunlight, awake and free
   from slumber couched in red
      to Butterfly's huge, flow'ry gaze
         and fragrant, blossomed head!

Be truth, your truth, and heaven sped!
   Oh, make my heart to know
      where Butterfly has gone to now,
         that I may also go!

Is she on wing to escape snow
   which lingers on the ground?
      Or, does she pass the time this day
         just flitting round and round?

I gather heather pound by pound
   to draw her ever near:
      but, just when I attempt to net,
         she turns to disappear!

Shine, Stars! Shine!

"Out of the depths" of my soul
   I have cried to you,
      oh, deep Lord!

But what are my depths? My whole
   being, through-and-through,
      rises toward

The one thinnest, flattest scroll
   in morn's mist of dew
      on a board!

―――――――――

"The heavens declare" the great
   glory of our King!
      Praise from mine,

Oh, Lord...from my gilded plate
   among the arched fling
      of design

From Your infinite template:
   glitt'ring, shimmering!
      Shine, Stars! Shine!

Carcass

I saw a gorgeous dragonfly
   upon the sidewalk: upside down,
      legs folded inward toward its chest,
         venational wings fully splayed.

I wondered that it caught my eye,
   since I'd already donned a frown!
      I envied it for finding rest:
         sequestration from life's parade.

A constantly-moving line of
   ants was visiting the carcass;
      dismantling it piece by piece, and
         carting it off to who knows where!

Out of sorrow and heartfelt love,
   I bent over, grasped (softly as
      I could) a wing between thumb and
         forefinger...stood up for a stare.

A few ants continued streaming
   out of its carcass. I puff-blew,
      so the ants ran out and either
         dropped off, or were given first flight!

You might think that I was dreaming...
   talking to the carcass, and, too,
      telling it my sorrow: neither
         it nor I could outlive our plight!

Ignominious death had found
  this, my brave fellow traveler...
    it no longer breathed, saw, tasted,
      felt, heard. It no longer flew through

Solar heated air...flitting round
  a branch, or the perfect flower.
    Certainly they haven't wasted
      time wondering about — with rue —

The dragonfly who used to pass
  by many times a day, seeking
    what, or where...no one really knows!
    I wondered how it met its fate;

Also, how death will encompass
  me. Will someone think of peeking
    at my carcass...as the ant goes
      forth with its piece of bread "in state"?

In its present condition I
  was far too late to give it a
    further, worthwhile lift. Still, I took
      it in the bier of my right hand

To a shady sphere (knowing I
  would have appreciated the
    thoughtfulness). I laid the "closed book"
      in tall grass...then withdrew my hand.

Cycle Two:

Death

If I Should Die

If I should die
   between the setting of the sun
     and the rising of the moon,
       don't wonder why
         darkness is so dark...can outrun
           the lunar dial's high noon!

Soon the moon's face
   will reflect vintage, brilliant light!
    Then huge, radiant morning
       dawns to erase
         the suffocating mask of night,
          exposing light's adorning

One!

Covered In Hearts

It cannot last, you know,
this pristine world covered in snow,
hid, not bidden to go
from the quiet, fireside glow
within our hearts.

How long have we stayed here:
snug, at rest, full of fluffy cheer
precipitate each year,
with a snowman pensive and near
who soon departs?

It gladly takes its turn
above, to better see and learn,
to stay, and so discern
the meaning of this brief nocturne
which ne'er restarts.

We must do just the same.
We've never had a rightful claim
On "Forever," by name.
Our rounds melt away, flesh and frame,
covered in hearts!

Death

By stealth I come.
You will neither see nor hear me.
The grave is my home.
My raison d'etre...to keep you always near me!

The Valley waits.
Its shadow never lifts, never shifts, never drifts along.
The inertial weights
of its black canopy and gates—impervious to love and even song!—

Hover, eternally hover.
And so there is no verdancy, no lushness, not a leaf.
Beneath Death's cover:
An occluded field beside a hidden cart bearing a never-gathered sheaf!

It Matters Not

It matters not if oceans surge
   and merge the earth's erratic ring;
      or stinging insects, trespassing,
         just zing the healing for their scourge.

It matters not if summer burns
   and turns the crops to darkest brown;
      or frowning winter blizzards down
         high mounds from heaven's frosted urns.

Each successive surging, merging,
   stinging, zinging, frowning, downing,
      burning, piles graying down. Frowning
         turns round...comes round...then lifts scourging!

Morning dew, and dying, too, soon
   festoon upwards to the azure
      realm...spurred through black clutter shuttered
         out: stirred arrays, prismatic boon!

It matters not if childrens' feet
   can't fleetly run to older years;
      or fears of "passing on" bring tears
         to eyes...lonely and sweet.

It matters not if killers dream
   to "ream" us all beyond repeat.
      They neatly go about their feat
         of cheating bravery through scheme!

Ev'ry precious child's feet beat,
   repeat on the golden street of
      God's love...where all can go: life's—love's—
         hard strifes are stopped there...and retreat!

Morning dew, and dying, too, soon
   festoon upwards to the azure
      realm...spurred through black clutter shuttered
         out: stirred arrays, prismatic boon!

You Must Leave Me Now

You must leave me now
where I sleep in the bow
of this tiny craft...
drifting far away, aft
of all I have known
and will yet know, yet own,
as the ship's breathing
sail—here, in the sheathing
gales; there, in wide strides
(meandering, slow tides)—
traces glitt'ring dunes
under peaked stars and moons!
You must leave me now
where I sleep in the bow...

You must leave me here
where I'm absent, but near
the holiest place:
pressing space with my face
and hands; seeing all
I ever dreamed of, all
I never thought of
as heavenly; above
the waterfall, distant,
but close; always instant,
yet beyond knowing
in full...ever growing!
You must leave me here
where I'm absent, but near...

<u>It Is Death</u>

K n e l l........................!
.
.
.

It is death,
and it is death's death:
taking breath,
and breath's breath; blocking
sight, and sight's
sight; deferring touch,
and touch's
touch; obscuring taste,
and taste's taste;
and squelching sound, and
sound's sound; then
fingering space, and
space's face,
and space's lace, and
space's space,
and space's place; while
fathoming time,
and time's chime, and time's
rhyme, and time's
climb, and time's time, and
time's time, and
time's time,
and

.
.
.

T i m e.............

I Didn't Want To Say Goodbye

I didn't want to say goodbye
  to all this:
    not the tears, the pain, and the hiss...
      I won't miss
        this ever in forever's sigh!

I didn't want to say goodbye
  to all that:
    not the pledge and its caveat...
      they're quite flat
        under the high, mushrooming sky!

I didn't want to say goodbye
  to all these:
    not the game, the jeers, and the tease...
      I'm at ease
        losing these in the by-and-by!

I didn't want to say goodbye
  to all those:
    not the sleepless nights, lost repose...
      I once chose
        this, that, these, those for my goodbye!

I didn't want to say goodbye
  to true you!

I Was Just Thinking

I was just thinking
   of life...always of life...
      and always of death, too.

I see a linking
   nexus flowing from life
      to death. There, death flows through

the narrow kinking
   back to expansive life:
      to sight, sound...back to you!

Always I'm drinking,
   gulping, guzzling your life
      from the clear sky-of-you!

Constricting, shrinking
   rites of passage—with strife—
      push me downward, down to

death's milieu: blinking
   past; future full of life...
      full of linear you!

I was just thinking
   of an hourglass: of life,
      and death; of a place through

which I'll be thinking
   only of your life, Wife,
      only of lasting you!

Cycle Three:
Virginia Tech., April 16, 2007

Before They Grew Old
Virginia Tech., April 16, 2007

A "day of infamy," to stand,
of the needs of the "bright" one
outweighing the needs of the
bland many...or, the few. His
hand, with white-hot metal,
has won! Done! The silver
dollar has spent his force.
He is corroding
neath vengeful ground...
thence to never misshis
stern appraisalby pissed,
minters in a far
deeper sheath!
I ache for them so! My
heart keeps wandering
to...fro, up...
down, looking for the
children, their leaps
of laughter by day, and
sleeps of smiling
peace; never a frown
by night or day. I didn't know
them, and yet, I did. Nothing
human is hidden (not one bow!)
from each of us: all below
God's heaven, and in God's
home, sing! Pray, sing of what?
Ah! Of life, death, love, joy,
hope, home, work, leisure...
and also, God. The
stag'ring breadth of His
birth, mirth, life, strife,
breath downing, uprising!
These are the cure for
ev'ry grief of heart,
and cleft *in loco*
parentis tolled.
It was
a greedy coward's
theft, leaving a
nation bereft!
They grew cold

b e f o r e   t h e y   g r e w   o l d!

V.P.I., April 16, 2007

He has done it again!
He has done it again!

The very same maniacal fiend
who, as a coward, publicity gleaned
by doing his dreadful deeds back then,
and now returned to keep us weaned
of brighter hopes from way back when.

He has caused me deep sighs!
He has caused me deep sighs!

Is this the brave and acceptable way
to tell the world, "I will not stay!"?
What right had he to bring sad cries
of dark anguish beyond today
from those whose child in stillness lies?

Shall I yet offer hope?
Shall I yet offer hope?

My own dismay should first be shared:
I faced the wall, and blankly stared.
What words can tell us how to cope?
I know! The answer is, we're paired
with all mankind: let us elope!

<u>Mother, Mother</u>

(This song was written March 3, 1985. The author now dedicates it to those whose lives were taken at Virginia Tech., April 16, 2007.)

Mother, Mother, come to me:
please tell me where a soul is free!
Is there a safe and peaceful place
to lose its fear, and leave no trace?

Mother, Mother, hear me now:
this ocean's found me, but I don't know how!
I'm in the strong undertow,
and soon my time must come, I know!

\>> Repetend <<

Mother, Mother, say a prayer:
remind me now that God is there
across this ocean surging still,
across this deep and lonely chill!

Mother, Mother, hold me near!
Make this cruel nightmare disappear!
Sing a sweet song that I may keep
before I sigh, and fall to sleep!

\>> Repetend<<

<u>Repetend</u>

Right when the moon is full and bright!
Just as the stars have filled the night!
Just as darkness engages light!
Right when I've finally found my sight!

Cycle Four:
Family

The Highways and By-Ways
(Have You Seen My Children?)

Have you seen my children anywhere?
I cannot find them at home!
Not sleeping in their rooms:
under blankets, o'er plumes
of pillows nestling curls
spinning all yarns of threads,
all threads of filaments;
shuttling recurrent dreams.
Oh! Their dreams—if 't were told—
would make all children gold,
glitt'ring as young Earth's gleams
couched among tenements
of stars tracing God's treads
and His sped roundhouse hurls
from the ends of light's brooms
sweeping neath infants' looms!
Have you seen my children anywhere?
I cannot find them at home!

<< Repetend<<

Have you seen my children anywhere?
I cannot find them at home!
Not sitting at table:
with family, stable,
mincing repartee's sharp
gibes with massed sibling tribes
full of laughter-and-song's
cornucopian splays
across the linen! Fold
the linen! For, when old,
full of glad harvest days,

't will bring thirsty throngs
of children for imbibes
from God's tall chalice-harp
strummed along each cable
strung from scripture's fable.
Have you seen my children anywhere?
I cannot find them at home!

<< Repetend <<

Have you seen my children anywhere?
I cannot find them at home!
Nót standing by the windows:
pointing to the hedgerows
of boxwood and holly
dangling plump, red berries
over deep mulch or snow,
waiting for sunlight, stars
lighting the winding road
leading away...back, towed
by the children's thick scars,
by the children's long row
of chinked, cobbled derring-
do 'cross life's wisdom, folly:
in chasms, up rainbows,
down valleys, through shadows.
Have you seen my children anywhere?
I cannot find them at home!

<< Repetend<<

Repetend

Please come with me out into the highways
and by-ways, that I may find my children,
and bring them home!

"Got That Happy Right!"

Mama was a sight, a sound, and an all-around character unlike anyone I ever knew! When she looked at you white fire flew from both eyes! No surprise! Honey, when that woman spoke, the flies awoke from their kind of slumber! And, be they wise (which they aren't), Mama always snatched them out the blue sky when they were flighty enough to wing it through the air past a hand and an arm which could rebound from her side quicker than a "squito" blinks...just found with new lashes never damped by the slightest dew! Child, if you think that's fast, now I've really got to tell you somethin' 'bout Mama: you could get one...two things off your mind pertainin' to work or the guys you work with, and if she agreed (meanin' no sighs!), Mama'd recite "Got that happy right!" before lies could ever have been *thought* by liars in a loo in England with nothing better to try and do than write on the stalls' walls...usually in blue! Let's not stop here! Mama'd out-hop a kangaroo when some idiot on the television clowned 'round with politics. If he could see how she frowned, sure 'nough he'd hit the ground, then hear Mama expound "Got that happy right!" before his dive made a pound!

<u>Brenda: Girl With A Twirl!</u>

Brenda is my sister, my twin...
   if you can even imagine
that! People always say to me
   that two of me, just two's like three
of anybody else! Then they
   say that "three is a crowd!" No way!
Not with "mwah"! First of all, I popped
   out four minutes before she dropped
(on her head, probably!). Second,
   I got the "looks" and the fecund
DNA! Which leaves her with what?
   I'm not quite sure! But, in a nut-
shell, Brenda has gumption! One day
   she stepped out on her back stoop, say-
ing, "I'm gonna shoot me a squirrel!"
   She raised her twenty-two, "Hurl Girl,"
fired, and hit one walking a
   line—a power line—at noonday!
Then, there was the impromptu twirl
   Brenda showed off, as a young girl,
in front of a motion-picture
   camera! "Girl With A Twirl!" sure
says it all for me 'bout my twin!
   Then, too, if we two argue, win-
ning is out of the question for
   me! Matter-of-fact, in the door-
way 's where you need to be if you're
   arguing with Brenda, 'cause, for
sure, there's only one person do-
   ing all the talkin': it's not you!
Then there's the lazybones aspect
   to Brenda's nature. You'll supect
her of worse things after I tell

    you this: years ago Brenda fell
onto the living room sofa...
    'bit tired. In moments, here came a
tick walkin' up her pants! "Twin Sis"
    pinched the critter, then—with great hys-
teria—placed it on my dog
    who happened by, dumb as a log!
Now, I mustn't neglect to men-
    tion Brenda's primary threat when
her husband makes her real mad. She
    shouts the following phrase, thusly:
"Two weeks!" You never saw a hard-
    headed man straighten up—a card
in the middle of the deck!—as
    fast as he does when Brenda has
that to say! "Two weeks!" That's all! Not
    one syllable more! The last knot
has been tied, then! Nothin' left to
    say but, "Okay, Brenda! You, too!"
One more thing: when Brenda decides
    to act, she moves with hastened strides;
I've known not to try and stop her
    "from knee-high to a grass hopper!"

Cycle Five:
Biblical Themes

The Prodigal

I gather that the morning found you well,
    you, Sparrow, perched there high atop the trees,
and list'ning to a summer's sylvan breeze...
    but gifting no one with your singing spell!

The Prodigal has seen you from the ground,
    and wonders why you've never come to rest
within his rough-hewn cabin-of-a-nest:
    a lonely place without a merry sound!

When autumn shudders down myriad leaves—
    red, brown, and hues infusing each other—
agape he stares, prepares for another;
    but just then it ends these tremulous heaves!

In winter, as the snow begins to fall,
    he knows, and goes where a cloister of white,
glittering throws pose except when his sight
    seems to melt away snowflakes, one and all!

Then, spring! Ringing, singing, bringing, green spring!
    His heart and soul dance like a butterfly
flitting to nature's bountiful supply
    of flowers, bowers...peace: that's the best thing!

Emmaus
(Mk. 16:12; Lk. 24:13-35)

Jerusalem stayed behind:
    deaf and blind, or sad and freightened...
It depended on the view
    of the few, or the stupid mob.
Midst their sobbing and despair
    (unprepared for the near future)
the allure of staying put
    with door shut, locked, captured the few.
Then, just two went for a stroll
    to a knoll with a small village.
Quirked visages made clear they'd
    heard news-trade of a turnabout.
The long, stout staffs in their hands
    evinced sands from many-a-walk
and long talk in desert lands.
    Making plans henceforth was but an
uncertain venture. All seemed
    surreal teamed with imaginings.
There are things past strange in life:
    some are rife with perplexity,
never free of mask and cloak;
    some, evoked by a sad sunset,
firstly met with tears and sighs,
    soon reprise even the sunrise!
So, baptized in mystery
    getting deep, dark, farther offshore...
the two ordained travelers
    made their first trip toward the Great Sea
since bold Peter rushed the grave
    of the brave Messiah's repose,
then stopped, posed a lean-to
    aslope new reason for poised hope:

linen rope—not wound round Christ!—
    tinged and spliced with spices and myrrh,
laid over on the cold slab
    in the drab, musty, rough-hewn tomb.
Soon, perfume from wild flowers
    (though flowers were never quite seen)
passed the screen of flared nostrils
    to tendrils of convolute thought.
The two sought the origin
    of the singular fragrance, but
quickly cut short the search, as
    a steep chasm seemed to echo
nearby. Lo! A still, small voice—
    just one!—choice as the surged sound-spree
of many waters, called them.
    Yet they stemmed their dull ears and minds.
Two near finds: fragrance and voice!
    But the choice to see, understand,
or just blandly pass along,
    right or wrong, comes to each of us.
Great faith plus prayerful action:
    these are fundamental to see
a true sea change conducive
    to our living with ears which hear,
eyes all clear. Now, a sea change
    in short-range of them, a stranger,
lithe and fervid, closed the gap.
    The soft clapping of his sandals—
intervals disclosing pace—
    took its place beside both of theirs.
But, immersed in discussion,
    the three shunned ev'ry percussion
of soles on bare feet. The man,
    whose gaze spanned eternal ages,
in stages stopped, totaling
    five, asking first, "Will you tell

me, as well as possible,
> what troubles you both through-and-through?"
Then the two, walking again,
> replied, "When Jesus, a prophet,
left hamlet and home to come
> here where some good could be done,
he was condemned to cruel death...
> his last breath taken on a cross.
What a loss! For our hopes were
> high and sure that he would redeem
the lost beam of Israel!
> How can hail fall from a blue sky,
and one's eyesight not catch it?
> Stone and flit assail ev'ry man!
So, how can a Jew go through
> all Jerusalem not bestirred
by the word of these hard pelts,
> and more?" Melts of compassion flowed
from the slowed and deeply moved
> man, who proved his wisdom under
this averring splash: "Ripples
> in barrels of wine or water,
like hail, surge briefly, then cease."
> The calm, peaceful stranger motioned
to stop anew. In due time
> he said, "Prime features of many
such pure delights elude their
> staunch seeker, as with the fragrance
and romance of wild flowers
> in bloom: stirs of Lily of the
Valley, of rose of Sharon.
> Then, too, under heaven, so few
will give true notice to the
> subtler utterances of each
human's speech. And now I must
> hear the thrust of your, 'and more.'

What things 'more' do you speak of?"
    Still west of the village, the
three caught up to where they thought
    they well ought to be. "Two long, dark
days have marked the time of his
    death, and this is the third," said one.
"But ere sun and blue sky were
    up, we heard some women insist
that the mist had not clouded
    their eyes. Predicating a claim—
that the same tomb where Jesus
    lay, now was empty!—they shared on
a vision of angels who
    shone right through the mist, and declared,
'Be not scared! He is alive!'"
    Then, depriving them of forward
motion toward the village (this,
    the third twist), the stranger beckoned
with his undulating staff:
    "O such daft and derelict fools!"
he said. "Pools of prophets soaked
    and resoaked you in these matters!
You seem cursed with dry, scaly
    unbelief! Of course Jesus died!
But this side of Glory could
    not, and should not keep him!" Claps of
his dust-covered sandals gave
    stark sound waves. So, the three ventured
on. The third stage was now past.
    For the last part of the slow hike,
it was like the synagogue:
    monologue citing scrolls of aged
and presaging holy writ.
    Hearing it, the two saw the way
that his sayings mirrored God's
    word; felt prods with which he appeared

to adhere it to himself.
    The bare shelf of understanding
now stocked, bringing them up to
    date, the two spotted the dotted
knoll (dotted with fireflies,
    nimbused eyes of candlelight, and
homes). A stand of sparsest palm
    trees, embalmed by a breeze from east
of, at least, the near Great Sea,
    chatted. The stranger halted there,
full aware that the pair of
    locals loved his company. (It
grew the pit of their small souls,
    causing wholesome verdure, and then
fruit!) Saddened by his fourth pause,
    and quite nauseated—vexed that
the man sat against the bark—
    both men marked his know silhouette
where the setting sun sent light
    against slight, overlapping dunes.
Life maroons us all from dark
    time to dark time. Surely, here sighed
the denied Maroon-of-the-
    world! With a bound to his tan feet,
softly greeting them, he took
    a step, looking eastbound, as if
to just sniff the air...travel
    on. Compelled by the lorn two to
stay, in lieu of passing town,
    settling down at the small, humble
table, culling bread, he blessed
    a loaf, stressed it with his scarred hands
until strands popped, parted fast
    (unlike past, *slow* parting-to-the-
base of the Sea of Reeds, when
    Moses sent shocked Israel through:

residues — salt, sand — on their
    feet). Ushering the dry, broken
chunks to tendered hands under
    their thunder-struck faces, he then
sought to engage them with prize
    ember-eyes, setting hearts ablaze!
So, amazed, they instantly
    knew Him! Seeing this, He vanished!
They, banished of all their doubt,
    looked about at each other, and
said, "How bland and blind we were
    till He stirred us up like coals, burned
in our yearning hearts, walked with
    us, talked with us, opened to us
long since, dusty passages
    'bout Moses and others in God's
enfilades of scripture! Yes,
    the Lord blessed us even before
we adored Him as alive-
    and-alive! Now, of course, after...
we've laughter again, having shot
    our bloodshot eyes first *to* Him, then
through Him!" When they'd said all this,
    they went missing...retraced the knoll,
the slow stroll, the whole matter,
    with the hurry of their quick sandals,
though the calls of the day filled
    to the hilt, already, much more
than a four-horse wagon could
    pull! And should they ever doubt Him
again, simple faith would turn
    them astern with reminiscing
and kissing such sights, sounds, smells
    as foretell something yet future...
something sure, with the allure
    of no cure on this dead planet...

something netting their souls for
> the great shore-to-the-greater-deck:
the elect Ship where there is
> One Who is Captain, Commander
of all! Or, put another
> way, brother, for now: the One Who
walked with two from the city
> toward the pitiful town...thus,
Emmaus!

Cycle Six:
Humor

"Up and Into the Bus!"

Paris Island:
many years it's been
since I fought hand
and foot to be seen

there...a recruit
in olive drab, hot
fatigues (the fruit
of some idiot

meddling in clothes
for jungle junkies
fighting "squitoes"
brought in by a "breeze,"

a humid mop
dropped on sweaty heads
like a bomb's plop,
or a monsoon's treads).

Oh, yes! I well
recall the dry fate
which soon befell
me there on that spate

of endless sand
neath the drill sergeant's
strident command-
voice: night raids on gents

like me who died
(so to speak) that day,
that "All denied!"
"Woe betied!" first day.

War is a bore;
war is just war; nay,
war isn't war
at all, when you stay

on that lone shore
where was the lone serg
who grabbed and tore
my heart like a barge

of true elites,
Force Recons: those "Retreats
don't happen!" treats;
sweet little, soft sweets

saving the world
by killing bad guys
lobbing unfurled
grief in their squint eyes!

The serg started
out by shouting, "Which
of you farted?"
We all laughed a stitch,

but the serge just
popped out another:
"What's funny? Trust
me, Boys, no other

stinking thoughts will
pass through you pursed minds
from now on! Fill
your minds—your land mines!—

with only that
with which I feed you,
or you'll go, 'Splat!'
like a crushed fondue!"

Not the first day,
but the first half-hour
marched the gray
timepiece to my bower!

Huh! My bivouac!
Huh! My tense ordeal
on the tarmac
(Death's mirage! Black steel!).

Inches from my
face poked the red, flared
nose of this guy:
neck outstretched, teeth bared,

barking at me
like I was stranger
than a donkey-
flea's hairy manger!

"What I say, you
will, too!" he said. (Well,
I *thought* this true.
But, thunderin' hell,

it wasn't true!
More accurately,
"What I say, you
will *do!*" correctly

states his cursed words!)
Without delay
he pushed forwards
to inveigh:

"Up and into
the bus!" Hearing my cue,
I yelled back to
him, "Up, and Into

the Bus!" Then he
cinched his angry face
like a sorry
prune, started to chase

me as I ran
for the bus: the bus!
My only plan
was to reach the bus

before the dude
reached me, breached me, then
waxed really rude,
or worse! Now, though, e'en

a "Rambo" could
not save my bad "mess"!
I was cooked wood!
Crispy! Under stress!

The "kill drill" sent
two corporals to
right my recent
wrong! We three just knew

someone wasn't
coming back out of
that bus! (Mustn't
cheat myself, though, of

some glory: I
tried so hard to harm
those two on my
firing range of arm-

bazookas! Still,
with all said and done,
I'd had my fill.
And they? They had won!)

Yet, to this day—
for all that great fuss!—
the sun's foray
into morning, well, jus'

makes me say: "Up
and into the bus!"

"Still Here!"

I cannot see you now,
neath this recumbent cow
engrossed in slimy cud
once rooted in the mud!

Although she knows I'm here,
she doesn't flick an ear,
nor even cease to munch
her clover by the bunch!

The masticating fool
develops a long drool
which seeps into the ground
where I am wholly drowned

inside this rotting trough:
no noise, not e'en a cough!
The dandelions grow
along the listing row

of headstones on display
where people come to pray
and listen for a sound
from underneath the mound

of a departed soul
beneath encroaching mole
which twitters just a bit
encountering the spit

mixed in the viscid sod
which never drinks of God,
just of me, and the rest!
Now, what is your request?

That I should be your guest,
fledged out this hidden nest,
this cup of resting ground
with fam'ly all around

our sound of joy's rebound?
You truly will astound
me if you'll but rebut
the facts encased in shut

cabinets in the earth,
among them, mine! Rebirth
is what you want? But, how,
above this bloated cow?

No, I cannot just rise
toward the open skies
retiring ev'ry day
aloft. But, where-away?

Nobody knows of this
mysterious abyss
where I shall go beyond
where you can, far beyond

the daylight's pointing spire!
Can you hear me? It's dire
under this chattel's ease
on mottled hide, and fleas!

Judicial ambiance
I want, but not a chance!
My words are muffled, gagged,
where justice has me tagged

beneath my bovine sin
with no support within
my brain and heart—just flat!
(and rightly so, at that!)—

where ev'rything I did,
worse, ev'rything I hid,
e'en ev'ry word I said,
yes, all those in my head

and life come back to find
me quite vacant in mind,
yet fully culpable!
Is there no lasting lull

just now to hide me from
the angel who will come—
soon come!—for me? And how!
I cannot see you now;

the angel stops so near!
Still, I would rather hear,
rather see, rather feel
where you've begun to kneel,

where we could laugh again
despite the frequent pain
of life, even with you,
my Love, even with you!

What shall I say or do
to loose the binding screw
which shuts me in this bin
of frigid night and sin

descending to their rest
within my sunken chest
which yearns for time—all time!—
to echo you clear chime,

your lilting vibrato's
opus more than all those
angels' songs, psalms, and sighs!
I want total reprise

with you, my Love; and then
we'll come here once again,
and lie together, downed,
after we've stood a round,

"To Bertha and her cud
atop the constant mud;
one life, one love, no fear:
Still here! Still here! Still here!"

Move Your Thumb!

Ouch! Where'd that pain come from?
    Dumb! Dumb! Move your big thumb

next time you make a ping
    under a way-back swing
        with that hard-headed thing,

that blunted claw-hammer!
    When you're "good" to slam her
        down, pause to look! "Whammer"
            must miss your large "jammer"!

You must certainly know
    that the very next blow
        won't go where it *will* go
            if you don't move your toe
                or your thumb! Sore dumb-bo!

Cycle Seven:
Christian Living

Praising God

What news today from far away
vesperal bells, or beached seashells;
from nearer glade, or promenade
deck ferried by the ocean's plod?

A knelled conclave, an echoed wave,
sweet solitude's heart-pounding moods
which never change nor rearrange
less than my sense of feeling odd.

If there is word, let it be heard
now and always, that all my days
originate, reverberate
abundant praise to raise to God!

Battling God

(John 3:30; Gal. 2:20)

I'm battling God.
Can you help me in the fray?
His reasoning is more mature
than anything I say!

The field is trod.
By the passing of each day
I've made a rank caricature
of war and war's foray!

On bloodred sod
my attempts to win...decay.
Now, I must yield to departure:
the only means to stay!

Strayed Far

I've strayed from the path again—
strayed far!—
from the good, from the sane,
from the guiding star!

I'm weighed in the balance pan,
weighed stripped
of my flesh, of my plan,
of the net I gypped!

I'd trade all my hopes and dreams—
trade all!—
for one day and the schemes
to avert recall!

A Lone Tree

A lone tree
high, looking straight back at crooked me,
into my eyes: convex filigree
arching inward, too, inward deeply;
tinted mirrors of the sky and tree;
Eden's clearest mirrors of light's three:
sun, moon, and stars, the sources (all free!)
of bright energy and synergy
for ev'ry person I know and see —
and for those I don't: such mystery! —
also the rainbow crowning fully
the lone tree
high, looking straight back at crooked me!

Calvary
high, looking straight back at crooked me,
into my eyes: concave filigree
arching outward, too, outward broadly;
tinted mirrors of my reaching-spree;
heaven's clearest mirrors of life's three:
Father, Son, and Spirit (Yes, all three!)
the sources of life's sure victory
for every person I know and see —
and for those I don't: such mystery! —
also the rainbow crowning fully
Calvary
high, looking straight back at crooked me!

Here Am Just I!

(2 Sam. 5:24; Isa. 6:8)

Was it a rustle of leaves I heard
atop the mulberry trees? Bestirred,
my heart lunges for the sky! Upward
go I to the high, stampeding herd
of whispers which say, "This is my word!"
Here am I, oh, Lord!
Here am just I!

What must I do that I may be true
to all You hold dear under the dew?
I'm seeing what others will not view;
I'm list'ning from heights completely new;
and my reasons swirl around full You!
Here am I, oh, Lord!
Here am just I!

Why should I spiral down by myself?
I'm used to it here, up in this shelf
of branches and leaves, and You Yourself!
I dare not go down! A "balmy elf!"
is what they will say; a "pompous self!"
Here am I, oh, Lord!
Here am just I!

It Will Sound Like A Boast

It will sound like a boast if I say
  that God loves me in a special way,
    and that I love Him with vigor's vim
      action and creative stratagem!

It will sound like a boast if I say
  that I pray throughout the lengthy day,
    that I regularly come away
      from prayer—from my encounter's close stay—

feeling much, much better, quite refreshed,
  no longer caught up, dragged, all enmeshed
    in life's dripping net out time's ocean,
      neath time's davit, without a good plan!

It will sound like a boast if I say
  that, all day, sometimes, the gentle sway
    of God's presence cuddles me in arm
      so soft—yet strong!—that I fear no harm!

It will sound like a boast if I say,
  often the miraculous display
    of God's hand on the earth, and in the
      heavens, makes me pause just to take a

moment or two to thank Him for all
  blessings: tangible, intangible!
    "The heavens declare God's great glory,"
      says the Book! Take a look: the Story

is true! I'm very grateful! Aren't you?
    One more thing I must say to just you:
        it will sound like a boast if I say
            that, throughout my life, and future's day,

God's love and presence dependably
    go with me: "through the shadow's valley,
        and valley's shadow! God is with me
            where no one else might potentially

come to my rescue! When life is through
    with me, God won't be! His ever new
        and infinite love will guide me to
            His "many mansions" beyond the blue,

bluer, bluest skies! My opened eyes
    will behold Him as ne'er before! Wise
        was I the day I said, "Yes!" to God!
            His tan, calloused feet already trod

this way before me! All I must do
    is hold His hand, as — like morning's dew —
        He surrounds and, too, saturates me
            with refreshment on my dry journey!

It will sound like a boast if I say
    that God is there — here! — as I, first, pray,
        then get on with my life! It's a boast —
            to which few would raise a heartfelt toast! —

to say that God's Third — the Holy Ghost —
    sails with me from, and to, ev'ry coast!
        In Him I live, and move, and have my
            being! Therefore, humbly, with an eye

toward sensibilities of others,
   I won't say what another's druthers
      might resent. It will sound like a boast
         to say things are this way! (Pssst! It's no boast!)

Cycle Eight:

<u>God</u>

Mr. Mystery

"Omnipresent," they say of God:
but I don't see; I don't feel; I don't hear
the "still, small voice" by which He is said to appear!
That blessed sound escapes my auditory enfilade!

And what of touch? Why not as much?
Oh, hold me in Your arms and tightly fold
this cold, lifeless, hard, and anthropomorphic mold,
as such, with true rapture, that I may know Your tactile touch!

Why prosecute these silly games
wherein the sole, the superlative prize
escapes all notice of my dust-encrusted eyes?
I stand woefully blind behind my shattered, convex frames!

Omnipresence

Are You there? Are You here
neath the splash of a tear,
o'er fragile atmosphere,
and everywhere between?

Yes? Then why do I lean
limply, and just careen
into languid and green
pea soup covered in kelp?

I only want Your help,
as a sib of a whelp
nuzzles, whimpers...no yelp!
Are You there? Are You here?

Cycle Nine:
Nostalgia

The Last Penny

Whatever happened to the dull penny
which was placed upon the railroad track
running through here, and north, for many
hoping that soon they'd venture back?

It was the last one in a deep pocket
of the boy who invested it there
with greater int'rest than a docket
has to a banker's line of care.

I never have seen such a lonely coin,
and it was positioned upside down:
the face—largely effaced—to conjoin
a final debasement in town!

Cycle Ten:

Fantasy

The "Solo Maiden"

I saw a passing ship today
    with larboard tilt, and starboard sway.
Sails in close proximity caught
    the briny gusts they ever sought,
till, nearing dusk, she made her berth:
    the "Solo Maiden" touching earth.

A gallant craft of seasoned wood
    with cracks which told of waves withstood,
and masts—as tall as cedar trees!—
    that pierced the sky, and sang the breeze!
She sallied forth in stately pride:
    the "Solo Maiden" on the tide.

But in my looking to the craft
    I saw no captain, fore nor aft;
helmsman watching, holding steady;
    seamen neath the yardarms, ready!
I saw a passing ship today:
    the "Solo Maiden" making way.

Just A Wish

Oh, that sky, high cloud, and bowed stars
could be true, newly found, renowned
exemplars—ours!—redolent, too,
of a breeze—please!—sent and spent, all

before Eve's sleeves—made of jade green
fig leaves grown, sewn by the Tigris—
firstly came: shame, sin within cloaked,
yet still here, clear naked! Naked!

Captain of the Seas

Tall sea, unfurling surge
   overwhelming this bark
      of humanity's splurge
         on the sea's disturbed arc:
            emerging demiurge

drifting, slowly drifting
   no place, some place, one place
      ultimately sifting
         vessels of lofty grace
            from low rafts ne'er uplifting,

listing landward, now aft
   yon crashing, surly hurl,
      yet netted in its draft,
         whirling above a pearl,
            atop an oyster's curved craft!

There's the ribbon, the beach
   and rocks, the scouring sand
      and pebbles! They will teach,
         or they will take; command,
            scuttle, or slowly breach!

Drawing nearer the shore:
   light-refracting shallows
      strewn with smashed slips of yore,
         shifting blues, drowned gallows
            birds prone to the ribbed floor,

Distillations

skeletal grounds in sync
   with eddies, long coral
      reefs of our beliefs, pink
         and antlered bones, floral,
            porous stones snagging—link-

by-link—sunken, engaged
   anchor chain and fluke. Wave
      heaving, humping, enraged,
         windward—as we—to stave
            our pulmonate cage gauged

with a straw. Heart's cargo
   of pride and sideward glance
      shifts leeward—embargo
         off—tilts, leaves a freelance,
            splashes and sinks ergo.

Roaring waves are quickly quelled.
   The inward tide lies asleep.
      A single bell, now, once knelled.
         Its toll was steep, did steep
            our deafened ears, and unjelled

our welled-up eyes: silent gongs
   weather-beaten by the sad
      spectacle (bodies on prongs
         snowed by swirled plankton; the mad
            debacle seen midst twirled throngs).

He comes! Captain of the Seas!
   His flagship sweeps from the kite-
      horizon to the squat keys,
         archipelagoes: blue, white,
            bobbing like boats; flattened lees.

He glides! His sails—'gainst the tide—
    inhale: billowed stride gaining
        on the capsized hull allied
            with ruination's straining
                visage, nearly under, spied.

He lowers away! Inside
    the lifeboat, neath the davit,
        sitting, grasping oars of tried
            oak pulled, then pushed (a habit
                from His youth), circling, astride

one keel, then one man dying.
    He lowers again; this time:
        broad hands, tough feet, and crying!
            Then He hoists, grapples—with prime
                forearm muscles—the sighing

child, puts him in the rocking
    cradle; ferries to the berth;
        moors; trundles him—with shocking
            speed!—aboard the "Tetra": mirth,
                and long, quiet days locking

end-to-end for days on end,
    months on end, years on end, seas
        on end—with a starboard trend!—
            making for Eternity's
                treasured, boundless spray on end!

"Tetra"? What's that? Her savored
    escutcheon, sign of these:
        faith, hope, love, these three! Favored
            Fourth? Eternity's release:
                Captain of the Seas! All 'board!

Cycle Eleven:

<u>Both Sides</u>

Dutch Door

One half was painted black.
One half was painted white.
One half was hanging back.
One half reached a new height.

One half was oiled and free.
One half squeaked noisily.
One half: a shut coffin.
One half: open often.

One half: hollow, breezy.
One half: solid, stolid.
One half: grimed, not queasy.
One half: washed, not squalid.

One half was hanging back:
this half was painted black.
One half reached a new height:
this half was painted white.
Black or white: never gray!

Makes me think of reasons:
only right, only wrong;
very simple reasons,
but only for so long!

Makes me think of tunnels:
inside, outside tunnels.
Makes me think of seasons:
hot, or freezing seasons.

Makes me think of penguins
flying under sky-ice.
Makes me think of sequins
squared and flecked like game dice.

Makes me think of tunnels:
inside, outside tunnels.
Makes me think of reasons:
very simple reasons.
Black or white: never gray!

She Dreams/He Dreams

She dreams of the ocean;
he, of wooden ships.
He dreams of commotion;
she, of tranquil quips.

She dreams of green meadows;
he, of higher ground.
He dreams of sheer hedgerows;
she, where blooms abound.

She dreams of petting cats;
he, of hunting deer.
He dreams of beer in vats;
she, "a smidgen, Dear!"

She dreams of flower sprays;
he, of plowing fields.
He dreams of horses' neighs;
she, some cackling guilds.

She dreams of soft moonlight;
he, of laser's power.
He dreams in black and white;
she, in a rose bower.

She dreams of spiral stairs;
he, of compasses.
He dreams of making chairs;
she, quilting classes.

She dreams of shopping sprees;
he, of staying home!
He dreams of bikes and skis;
she, of staying home!

She dreams of many maids;
he, of doing all!
He dreams of crack brigades;
she, of doing all!

She dreams of taking trips;
he, of going back!
He dreams of flirty lips;
she, of going back!
She dreams of show'ring gems;
he, of sluicing gold.
He dreams of diadems;
she, of castles old.

She dreams of staying young;
he, of oaken canes.
He dreams of staying young;
she, of higher planes.

She dreams of all that's sung;
he, of voiceless chimes.
He dreams of straw and dung;
she, refreshing climes.

She dreams of Taj Mahal;
he, of building homes.
He dreams of farm and stall;
she, flowerpot loams.

She dreams of published books;
    he, the ink and all.
He dreams of fishing hooks;
    she, the midnight ball.

She dreams. He dreams. They dream:
    they, of each other;
    they, of love's brightest beam
    unlike another!

Metal and Mineral

Metal is extracted from
   mineral kidnapped at home,
      at rest; at best, conjugal
         with stone—rarely free to roam—
            captive, hidden, internal.

Not that mineral is dull:
   its great outcroppings and full
      massifs always interject
         a mother lode sluiced to cull
            the dull...to shine and inspect.

Metal is leeched from the ground,
   bled from veins (crooked, not round),
      drained from cavities and cracks,
         pooled in molds, and cooled (no sound),
            settled where it may relax.

Not that mineral won't melt:
   molten igneous. To smelt
      it takes lots of heat and glow
         to know the quality held
            inside exterior flow.

Cycle Twelve:

Life

Depression

I have been here before,
    this place of shadows and lines,
        cracks, crevices, abandoned mines;
            of fissures hissing, pissing steam,
                and the thund'rous rolling of a beam
                      tossed across an upper, wooden floor!

I have been here before,
    this place of barnacles, rust,
        oil, bilge water, foaming gray crust;
            of dirty bottles drifting by,
                and murky eddies of schooling fry
                      born to this, and nothing, nothing more!

I have been here before,
    this place of dampness and fog,
        scum, slime, sludge, and a stifling bog;
            of strange forms in cumulus clouds,
                and dormant pupae in cocoon-shrouds
                      being eaten through a widened pore!

<u>Time To Go</u>

Masticated my herds of sheep and cows;
    imbibed my river of drinking water;
        cremated cords of trees in a slaughter;
            penetrated the earth with blood and ploughs.

Traversed millions of miles on painted roads;
    read through long, deep files of boring paper;
        rose to the summit of a sky scraper;
            looked down on the vagabond's bundled load.

Punched in at the clock all specified hours;
    dripped out of my brow the tally of sweat;
        moderated lies of the tv set
            neath acres of truncated wild flowers.

<u>Orphaned</u>

The great ones are all gone!
The great ones are all gone!
The patriarchs and matriarchs;
the magisterial monarchs;
the chosen few (but others, too)
who—visiting like morning's dew,
soon vaporized into the blue—
have left us dry as desert bone,
and full of woes in place of few
whose glory filled our reddish dawn!

<u>Do You Suppose...?</u>

Do you suppose that barred rainbows—
   arching through the azure—
     bend, no end, as a circle goes,
       midst high bump and wide blur
         of the atmosphere?

Do you suppose that mountain tops—
   pushing upward, upward—
     venture in oozed, igneous plops
       downward, downward, toward
         the interior?

What is life but some rainbows
   and mountains: both highs and lows?
     Life cannot keep the plateaus
       for long! In short, living goes,
         I rightly suppose!

Do you suppose that sunlight's beams
   stream in both directions, and thus
     are reflected back to their seams:
       an invisible omnibus
         making endless rounds?

Do you suppose that tides come in,
   then wander back out? An equal
     turnabout? Flow, also ebb? Win,
       and lose? Give and take? Conjugal?
         Nature's losts? Also nature's founds?

Distillations

What is life, but some sent beams
  and tides: both in and out streams?
    Life cannot, must not ply schemes
      ahead. In short, time for dreams,
        I rightly suppose!

Where Do You Sleep?

Inside a palatial house?
Beside a gutter-wet mouse?
Out on a vast, open plain?
Sprawled across a steamy drain?
Under nightly, sparkling skies?
On a roof, with smog-filled eyes?
Crammed in a tight cubby hole?
Deeper? Beneath a snug mole?
On a bed in the spread dead-
of-night? Wide awake with dread
of the future...the brief flit
of humanity's moonlit
cruise? We choose! Both you and I
must decide...choose where to lie,
where the patchwork quilt of life
will cover us in the end:
beneath disastrous buy...spend?
Or, above a golden heap
of faith, hope, love: all to keep
forever whether prostrate
in earth, or reposed, elate
in Christ's Majesty, lids closed,
sealed, sunk, hollow, decomposed;
seeing still the seamless quilt
on Christ's springy mattress — gilt
with colors of ev'ry hue! —
musing on His blessed, true
respiration; peace, joy, sighs
eternal in Paradise!

In A Dream

In a dream:
    in a dream, I see all
        so clearly;
           not nearly
                as confused am I
                    in a dream!

When I wake:
    when I wake, clarity
        is all gone;
           the bright dawn
                darkens my blue sky,
                    when I wake!

Shall I, then, sleep, or arise?
Shall I, then, keep or open my eyes?

Which is better? Which worse?
Which will fetter? Which disperse?

Living hurts and bemuses!
Dying flirts with, then abuses!

We Each Have A Closet

We each have a house, a room,
and a closet.
No question here, where the broom
cannot posit!

What is cringing neath the pole
in your cubby?
Pursuit of some naive soul,
lovey-dovey?

Hatred: bitter, vengeful, cruel,
still pursuing?
Greed like a sponge in a pool,
never spewing?

Ahhh! You cannot get away
from this tight space!
Sooner, or later—let us say—
comes much disgrace!

Have you tried that basket's nest
of wicker? Porous
as a showgirl's brain! Obsessed
as her chorus!

Perhaps the padlocked, old trunk!
It's a neat sight:
full of nothing but your junk;
unhinged, not tight!

There's the shelf of shoes and "sneaks"
under the plastic
where nobody ever peeks
'cept "Jurassic"!

No! No! No! No hiding it
where no one looks!
Closets always "threesome" it,
like grappling hooks!

What is a reformed sinner
to do about
that "thing" hidden far inner?
Just throw it out!

<u>My Friends</u>

(For Mike and Sandra Brinkley)

My friends are they
   who always say
      they love me!

My friends are two
   who never flew
      above me!

We fly a vee
   with none of three
      at the point!

It's God Who's there
   to face and bear
      the wind's joint

Pussssssssssssh! And Pullllllllllllll!

Cycle Thirteen:
Anecdotes

The Most Beautiful Instrument

Many, many years ago
I asked a sage to declare
which musical instrument—
midst all others, finely tuned—
was the most beautiful, crooned
by hand's command implement:
fingers! (They linger here...there,
till eyes arise, and hearts glow!)

Not a moment did it take
before he gave his answer:
experienced, well thought out,
succinct, distinct, and good prose
that an aged, great man knows.
Let all those who would cast doubt
on him—as a free lance—sure
pocket the tongue, and awake!

He stated: "The human voice,
without question, settles it
irrefutably! Oh, yes!"
And I, standing there amazed,
raised an eyebrow, and he gazed
as though I'd made a rank mess!
So I calmed down a wee bit,
and accepted his wise choice!

"The Size Of That Thing!"

I was living in a northern state,
a Yankee planning to move south,
conflate my life in the "Garden State"
with the "Old Dominion('s)" Plymouth—

Jamestown—and places farther inland.
I paid a man one hundred bucks
to drive me from there to here, in hand
with what is often borne on trucks!

It was hot and humid, just steaming
like a Turkish bath! We, sweating
till the ooze formed rivulets streaming
in our eyes, off our chins, vetting

every pore in our bodies, live-
puddling on the seats and floor as
we made our way down I-95,
headed, first to my sister's grass

in a rural town called, "Farmville." Yep!
I said, "Farmville"! Hub of three spokes:
Buckingham, Cumberland, and the dep
of Farmville (Prince Edward) when folks

still ran the train through there. Anyway,
here we come, Lloyd and I, onto
the dusty, gravel road where the hay
was tall as a skyscraper's new

flagpole! We crept—open windows—down
this long, snakelike road with our load,
when we were invaded by the frown
of an insect, fat as a toad,

and longer than the tongue of a cow!
Flying, flitting about the car
as though not knowing where to go now,
she covered the windshield's radar

screen with venational wings wider
than a venetian blind! Lloyd flailed
at the thing like a drunken spider
dangling from one filament bailed

out of a free-spinning spinneret
just above a hungering frog!
The car swerved from ditch to ditch, then met
a farmer's pickup-with-a-hog!

We skinned by that poor, future rasher
which oinked when Lloyd battered the bug
down off the glass, onto the dash: her
bulbous, striped eyes not worth a plug,

yet, seeming to glare with a set stare!
Lloyd, wide-eyed, and with shouting zing,
asked me this one question with a scare:
"Did you see the size of that thing?"

I guffawed, but Lloyd couldn't do it!
His response to that creature's stark
measurements reminded me a bit
of the movie named, "Jurassic Park"!

Distillations

Epilogue: To make matters far worse,
when Lloyd and I drove up the drive,
my little nephew spoke a brief verse.
Squatting in a plastic pool's dive,

Jesse yelled to me (leaving the car),
"Uncle Brent, look what we're having
for supper!" Then, like a rising star,
he got to his feet, hands having

a string of freshly-caught, large crappie!
Needless to say, Lloyd didn't stay
for dinner! He was quite unhappy!
He "packed it in" and sped away!

To my knowledge, he hasn't come back
to Farmville's bugs, fish, railroad track!

Cycle Fourteen:
Ways of the World

Making Juice

See the presses pressing out the juice
of fruits: some ripe, easy to reduce
    to pulp, not to be gulped like a moose
      guzzles from the Crystal River loose
        along orchards worked by a recluse
          whose weathered hands,tanned by ray abuse,
        maneuver adroitly to produce
    a harvest to be taken for use
      where trundlers of long-stemmed glass deduce
    the abstruse merits—clarets, vermouths—
of age, soil, climate; all to induce
pleasure: several kinds, no excuse!

Cycle Fifteen:
Evolution

It Isn't the Same, Now!

It isn't the same, now,
now that the cow has "come home to roost,"
and the rumor mill has long deduced
a myth called, "Evolution"! Its wild
theory is that you were not a child
millenia ago, or so! So
God was never here below the show
in the big sky where some "big bang" made
the heavens and the earth, which then made
accidents of birth, like you (later,
not sooner) whose slow incubator
combined aeons and chance alongside
mutation's "advance" in a half tide
flowing in, higher in, never out!
It moves God out, still brings Man about!
Through freak regression—"evolution"—
there's been a linked, chained revolution
in our minds, which makes me have to say,
"It isn't the same, now, any way,
now that the cow has "come home to roost,"
and the rumor mill has quite traduced
Creation here and now!

Cycle Sixteen:
Shaped Poems

I Drop

(John 3:30; Gal. 2:20)

<pre>
                    I
                    II
                    III
                    IIII
                  Chiink.
                ChinkChink.
              Chink.....Chink.
             Chink............Chink.
            Chink.................Chink.
           Chink......................Chink.
          Chink.............................Chink.
         Chink..................................Chink.
          Chink....Chink....Chink.....Chink....Chink.
        Chink...Chink....Chink...Chink....Chink....Chink.
      Chink...Chink..Chink...Chink...Chink..Chink...Chink.
     Chink...Chink...Chink....Chink.....Chink....Chink...Chink.
   Chink...Chink...Chink...Chink..Chink...Chink...Chink...Chink
   Streeeeeeeeeeeeeeeeeeeeeeeeeeeeeeeeeeeeeeeeeeeeeeeeeeeam.
   Puuuuuuuuuuuuuuuuuuuuuuuuuuuuuuuuuuuuuuuuuuuuuuudle.
   Flooooooooooooooooooooooooooooooooooooooooooooooooo
   oooooooooooooooooooooooooooooooooooooooooooooooooow.
   Riiiiiiiiiiiiiiiiiiiiiiiiiiiiiiiiiiiiiiiiiiiiiiiiiiiiiiiiiiiiiiiiiiiiiiiiiver.
   Flooooooooooooooooooooooooooooooooooooooooooooooooo
   ooooooooooooooooooooooooooooooooooooooooooooooooood.
       Roooooooooooooooooooooooooooooooooooooooooo
          ooooooooooooooooooooooooooooooooooooar.
            GOOOOOOOOOOOOOOOOOOOOOOOOO
               OOOOOOOOOOOOOOOOOOOOO
                  OOOOOOOOOOOOOOOO
                     OOOOOOOO
                        OD!
</pre>

Eve and Adam

She:
naked, but unaware
that she was wholly bare—
or barely bare in light
of innocence—came right
from Adam's rib (the site
of Woman's first waking
from exigent taking
of sleep and bone, making
life possible, aching
for a brief while). What joy
Eve brought to Adam's foy
for bachelorhood's coy
reticence (an alloy
of pride and a child's toy).

He:
Adam, naked—but not
concerned either, quite hot
for growths of innocence
planted in lush Eden's
garden midst the cadence
of a river flowing
to Havilah's glowing
gold—first saw Eve showing
in God's hand, nudged, slowing
as she neared the struck man.
"Bone of my bones! A plan
most beautiful! Woman-
in-the-flesh!" crooned the man.
"Helpmeet! Wife! Best of man!"

Bubbles Of Laughter

Round me it adheres! mini cosmic ears
Sound of bubbly cheers: of Time's chimes and gears
undulating spheres, orbiting the years,
    circumjacent clears,   stellar engineers
   compact atmospheres,   of orbs in high tiers
  convex, concave peers,   ahead...in our rears,
    drifting chandeliers,   fragile souvenirs,
bobbing boutonnieres,   ethereal tears,
global prism-smears,   circumflex veneers
  circumscribing seers,   capturing frontiers
       orbicular biers,   of concentric sheers,
    viscid hollow meres   ringed aeons and years,
    whirling grenadiers, seamless hemispheres,
  spraying bombadiers, see-through matched brassieres,
      effervescent piers buoyant blown halteres,
      holding midst all fears, laryngeal veers—
      tranquil mutineers, popping in my ears—
      bouncy gondoliers, my heart so reveres!

<u>Going Backward</u>

I see snow
      falling...
            falling...
                   falling.

I hear snow
      calling...
            calling...
                   calling.

Yet, to my shame,
            I have not followed its pristine trail!
            I have not answered its gentle "Hail!"

                I am frozen in my track
                which winds—not forward—
only back.

            Oh, to have chosen a different tack

                  than always
            stalling...
      stalling...
stalling!

Cycle Seventeen:
Romance

Eternally Yours!

Now that the time has come
    for me to go
        from all I know
            to depths and heights which will

flow in one direction—
    as linear light,
        and time's straight flight
            (never round or discrete)—

slight, I leave you strong love:
    a one-time gift
        bearing no shift,
            eternally yours, though!

...Only For A Moment?

    Is there no lull, no break
        from this costly "mistake"
            I've made: this loving you—
                no other!—as I do;
                    this strolling in hard rain
                        midst sheltered, with'ring pain;
                          this veined-granite pleasure-
                              in-the-rough heart treasure;
                              this fine, gritty, tan sand
                                  my hand clutches—first fanned—
                                  clasping e'en the tarnished,
                                    ornate chest spilling garnished
                                      streams out its weathered tent
                                      ...only for a moment?

I Didn't Want To Say Goodbye

I didn't want to say goodbye
   to all this:
      not the tears, the pain, and the hiss.
     I won't miss
       this ever in forever's sigh!

I didn't want to say goodbye
   to all that:
      not the pledge and its caveat.
     They're quite flat
       under the high, mushrooming sky!

I didn't want to say goodbye
   to all these:
      not the game, the jeers, and the tease.
     I'm at ease
       over these in the by-and-by!

I didn't want to say goodbye
   to all those:
      not the sleepless nights, lost repose.
     I once chose
       this, that, these, those for my goodbye.

I didn't want to say goodbye
   to true you!

Love's Stirring At Sea!

Churning! I'm churning!
    I'm lost in this long, engulfing pour:
        above the ocean's floor,
        beneath the tidal bore,
        submerged forevermore
in currents flowing o'er the low shore
    of love's new learning!

Spinning! I'm spinning!
    I'm spun in this dancing waterspout:
        spiraled in and about
        the cyclone's turnabout,
        vaulting upward, throughout
raring, flaring hurls and whirls that flout
    all but love's winning!

Have you no flat sea?
    Is the sand of my heart not gritty
        enough for your city
        of sky, sea, and flitty
        visitation's pretty,
inundating, gyral density?
    Love's stirring at sea!

I'll Take This Chance!

Lovely tonight: the moon,
the stars, and you—
gorgeous!—just passing through
the courtyard boon

of high-hanging gardens
like Babylon's
great wonder drinking ponds
out water's wends

from the Euphrates, south
to the Tigris
confluence, thence to kiss
the salty mouth

of the Persian Gulf's "tongue"
bounded by the
clean, sparkling, ivory
sands as the strung

stars we see here tonight!
I'll take this chance
to ask you for a dance
under this sight!

I Can't Close My Eyes Again!

Was it only yesterday
    that the sun and convex sky
        came together as an eye?
            Blueball! Pupil: bright as gold
refined seven times a day!
                Never ever growing old!
Open always 'long the way!

Still, the universe won't do
    as the socket of my love
        looking on you from above
           with all the angles I make
in a twinkle's shiny, new
              dawn: glistening in its wake!
I just want to stare at you!

No! The universe's space
    can't contain all that I see
        and feel about you...can't be
           nearly large enough to fit
the visions I can't displace
              from my mind's eye which is lit
in split seconds by your face!

I can't close my eyes again...
    not to blink, or think a "sec"!
        Though a quick, galactic fleck
           draw a bead upon my lids;
though an orb shoot as light's train
              toward my corneas...no skids;
never close them! Not again!

Or Am I? And Do I!

I didn't mean, Love, that I
   would never die,
      having promised you the sky!
      It is eternal, not I!
      Or am I?

The sky, Love, I mean to give
   you while I live:
      high, but ever nigh, blue sieve
         straining not the heart I give!
      And do I!

It's Lovely Here With You!

It's lovely here with you,
    like two close deer above
        a dove-like, sheer cascade!
            Afraid to veer closer,
                closer your cheerful voice —
                    no choice this near! — I'll kiss
                        your glist'ning, dear, sweet lips!

It's special in this place,
    your face within my reach:
        a beach, a cove of stars!
            Yet ours will win a view
                all new: our singular
                    love — bar none! — twin of no
                        rainbows spanning earth's slips!

It's privileged where you look,
    a book: a fairy tale
        of sails foursquare making
            for springtime air and sky!
                And I, I'm rarely seen
                    between my stares at you,
                        yours through me: careless trips!

Where?

Where is the autumn leaf
    which spiraled to the ground
    in a molt of color,
        brief, but louder than sound?

Where is the surged water
    which plunged into the pool:
    from a splash to fuller
        merging...tranquil, and cool?

Where is my truest dream
    which awoke me from sleep...
    from drowsy, wan pallor:
        gleaming, painting my deep?

Cycle Eighteen:
The Rapture

"Light Through Night!"

If you could but think of me
   as a man of hopes and dreams,
     then, simultaneously,
        I would wish you bright moonbeams
           bouncing off the old man's face,
              not trapped where gray pockmarks squat,
                 shuttling sunlight without trace,
                    come to offer all they've got:
                       light through night!

So much emptiness between
   the lunar surface and here:
      a vast, uncovered tureen,
         invisible, and quite blear—
            (as life itself is, often)—
               even worse: lonely and dark.
                  Then we go to our coffin,
                     waiting for the trumpet's bark:
                      "Light Through Night!"

"Please Come!"

    Will you visit my grave
each day
    in the hushed cemetery, or nave,
to pray?

    I still will need your roves
above
    its secluded, denuded, lost trove's
deep cove,

stranded, marooned, banished
    like John
on Patmos: all else ebbed, drained, vanished,
    just gone

to familiar coasts, with
    no thought
for my posthumous, alluring myth
    not sought

where sea anemones
    yet grow
upward, outward, seaward in the lee's
    ebbed flow,

later swelled to implore,
    "Please come!
I shall wait, watch, standing on the shore!
    Please come!"

Will you visit my grave
    each night...
in the hushed cemetery, or nave,
    contrite?

I still will need your joy
    beside
cloistered, quiet, lonely, frugal foy
    supplied

by skeletal hands neath
    hollow,
black cowls and pleats gliding to bequeath,
    follow

rank-and-file zombies' gowns
    to realms
mysterious, haunting chants, and frowns,
    stuck helms,

masters and commanders,
    lashes
flicking every fly from votive
    ashes

wafting upward, spelling,
    "Please come!
I shall wait, tend the Bride's dwelling!
    Please come!"

Cycle Nineteen:

Winter

"It's Cold! Freezing!"

The days are shortening, and
still shortening,
just like summer's quick remand
of lingering
chill in spring's clinging air band:
rising, falling
again in the grayish land
shrug-shuddering
autumn's fling of leaves, like sand,
from shivering
earth's   round-shouldered,   barren   stand
of quick-twigging
trees now shamefaced 'long their grand
boughs pretending
not   to care   that   men sing   and
rake: not   blushing
except when feeling the fanned,
leafy   rustling
bringing winter's vocal command:
"It's   cold!   Freezing!"

This Christmas Morn

♥
O V
L   E

from the music box fed, nor a tray swelled round
nor a merry sound by warm ginger bread,
with some shiny thread,   nor the fireside drowned
nor a gift all bound   in a wavy red,
neath an angel spread,   love will still surround
though no tree be found   you and crown your head
when you rise from bed,   with a jeweled mound
This Christmas morn   of my thoughts unsaid!

Printed in the United States
200385BV00006B/455/A